RASCHE NOTATION 2

Write your Argentine Tango dance phrases

Thomas Rasche

Rasche Notation 2
Write your Argentine Tango dance phrases
Thomas Rasche

ISBN 978-1-4461-4250-9

First published in July 2010. Published by Thomas Rasche.
Print and distribution by Lulu.com

Thomas Rasche, Suite 105, 179 Whiteladies Road, Clifton, Bristol BS8 2AG, UK. Email: thomas@RascheNotation.com
www.RascheNotation.com

If you would like to publish your own notation on the web, add this logo to your website as a link to the Rasche Notation homepage at RascheNotation.com. This will help other people find out more:

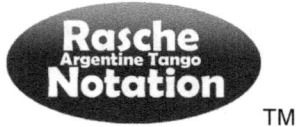

TM

The above logo is copyright and trade mark belonging to Thomas Rasche. It may only be reproduced on a website as a remotely sourced image, linking to the website www.RascheNotation.com, and used within the context of dance notation.

Credits
Covers and Buenos Aires Congresso sketch by Thomas Rasche. The front cover image is based on a photograph by Loukia Lili, taken at an *assado* (grill evening) in Bath, UK in May 2008. Dancing in the rain are Thomas Rasche and Catherine Garrett.

You can discover more about Rasche Notation

Rasche Notation book
The original in-depth description of Rasche Notation, including background, information, examples and more.
Published March 2009.
ISBN 978-0-9561489-0-2

Rasche Notation notebook
Write full choreographies on pre-printed blank staves. A4 format.
Includes a RaNote summary of symbols.

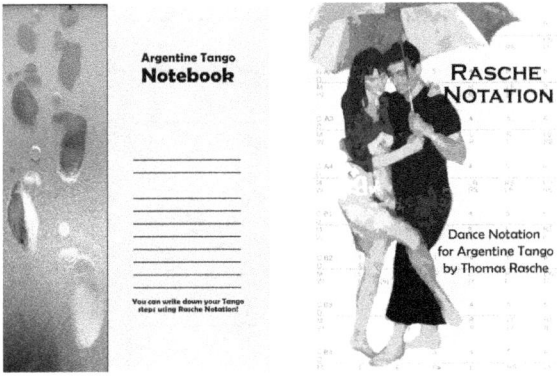

Both these books are available online:
www.RascheNotation.com

This website also includes links and current information about Rasche Notation. You can find discussion forums and more...

1   **21**

    22

    23

    24

    25

    26

    27

    28

    29

2   **31**

    32

    33

    34

    35

    36

    37

    38

    39

4

Contents

Rasche Notation 2 (RaNote2)

To write dance phrases, we first need an easy way to write steps...

Steps
Steps are written by describing destinations (using text symbols). The symbols combine using the syntax: 'what goes where'.

Writing is reduced as much as possible by using assumptions. For example, we assume readers can dance Tango, lead and follow. It is assumed that every step is completed: the step is taken <u>and</u> the axis/ weight is fully transferred onto/ over the placed foot.

L,R are abbreviations for the **L**eft and **R**ight feet (or legs). They typically form the 'what...' part of the syntax.

Dance steps are mostly taken around the partner. Imagine a circle drawn around the partner, the width of the embrace (in the diagram between * and *). Steps are placed on this imaginary circle. There are three types:

S,B,F abbreviate three steps: **S**ide step (also called an open step), **B**ack cross step (across and behind the standing leg) and **F**orwards cross step (in front and across the standing leg). These are typical '...where' steps.

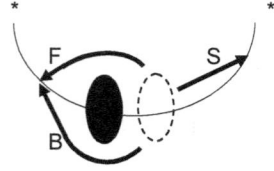

s,b,f These are small steps, with the feet together. **s** is a close (**s**ide) step. **b** and **f** are small cross steps in directions of **B** and **F**. E.g. the woman's cross step (*trabada*) is written **Lf**.

+, − If a step is towards a partner (not onto the imaginary circle) **+** is added. A step away from the partner **−** is added.

Now combine these symbols... and many steps can be written!

Examples using **L**,**R** (what…) together with **S**,**B**,**F** (…where):

LF   **L**eft foot does a **F**orwards cross step.
RB   **R**ight foot does a **B**ackwards cross step.
LS   **L**eft foot does a **S**ide step.

Examples using **L**,**R** (what…) together with **s**,**b**,**f** (…where):

Lf   **L**eft foot steps so that the left leg is crossed in **f**ront of the standing (right) leg, with the feet touching. This is how to write the woman's cross step (*trabada*).
Rb   **R**ight foot steps **b**ehind, but touching, the left foot.
Ls   **L**eft foot steps to a close position, to the **s**ide of the right.

Examples of **+ −** (…where) used after the other symbols:

L+   **L**eft foot (what…) steps towards (**+**) towards the partner (…where).
R−   **R**ight foot steps away from the partner.
RS−   **R**ight foot steps **S**ideways and away (**−**) from the partner (a back-right diagonal step).

Special steps
Special steps have a particular (…where). These destinations can be described by adding relevant symbols:

%   step between partner's feet (**%**).
=   Touching (**=**), assume with partner's foot.

Examples of special steps:

L%   **L**eft foot (what…) steps between (**%**) partner's feet (…where).
LF%   **L**eft foot does a **F**orwards cross step, between the partner's feet (**%**).
R=   **R**ight foot touches (assume partner's foot)

Incomplete steps

Each step is assumed to be complete. This means it includes all of the following: collect of the free foot (bringing it towards the balance point), followed by its projection/ placement, then partial weight transfer, and finally full weight transfer onto the foot. If a step is incomplete, it finishes early at one of these points. This can be described, with an additional symbol:

c	**c**ollect. The foot is brought in, next to the standing leg.
p	**p**lacement. The foot is projected and placed on the floor.
r	partial weight transfer (**r**) onto the placed foot.
n	full weight transfer (**n**) onto the placed foot.

Non-step movements

Any other movements, other than the steps above, can be described using the same syntax. These are less frequently used, as these describe extra movements beyond those needed for the steps. Here are some non-step (what...) symbols:

@	Free leg movement (movement in the air, without being placed on the ground). If it's without a (...where) symbol, see context, or assume leg takes a long route (stretched).
¥	Embrace/ torsion. If it's without a (...where) symbol, assume torsion straightens & emabrace shape resumes.
€	To lead. Without a (...where) symbol, assume the leading is such that the partner can do the steps as described.
Ω	Legs (i.e. lower part of the body, from the waist down).
Φ, Ø	The axis (**Φ**). Leaning axis (**Ø**), without a (...where) symbol, assume towards the partner (**+**).

Here are some more (...where) destination and information symbols, that are typically used with non-step movements:

C,G	**C**lockwise, and anticlockwise (**G**).
↑	up, or a step over.
gan	Words can also be used to describe a destination or type of movement. For example, words can describe a **bol**eo or **gan**cho.

Examples of incomplete steps, using **c**,**p**,**r**,**n**:

LSr   **L**eft foot does a **S**ide step, and part weight transfer (**r**).

Rc   **R**ight foot **c**ollects. Compare this to **Rs**, with the same finish location, but Rs <u>is</u> a complete step with weight put onto the Right foot after it is collected and placed.

nR   the weight is fully transferred (**n**) onto the **R**ight foot (remember the syntax 'what'=n goes 'where'=R).

R%r   **R**ight foot steps between (**%**), and part weight transfer (**r**).

c   **c**ollect. The context will describe which leg is collected.

LSp   **L**eft foot does a **S**ide step. It is placed (**p**) without weight.

Examples describing the free leg, using the **@** symbol:

@   Free foot (**@**). If there is no **L** or **R** symbol, see the context for which leg it is. If there is no (...where) symbol, see the context for movement info.

L@b   **L**eft free foot (**@**), moves to **b**ack cross position. It is not placed: it is a free leg.

R@f   **R**ight free foot (**@**) moves to **f**orwards cross position. It is not placed: it is a free leg.

L@s   **L**eft foot (**@**) moves to a **s**ide close position, without weight transfer: it is a free leg.

L@B   **L**eft free foot (**@**), moves to a **B**ack cross step direction. The capital letter suggests the distance is further away, for a bigger movement. This is one way to write a *boleo*. Alternative: **L@bol**.

R@%   **R**ight free foot kicks between partner's legs (**@%**). It is not placed: it is a free leg.

Note, symbols **c** and **@s** describe exactly the same movement: the free foot is collected to the side of the standing foot. They are both included in RaNote for completeness, described either as part of a step, or as a free leg movement. If the movement is anything other than a normal collect, the **@** should be used, followed with the movement information.

Compare **c** and **@s**, to the symbol **s**. All end in similar positions, but **s** is a step, so weight <u>is</u> transferred onto the placed foot.

RaNote stave

So, now that we can write steps, we can use these to write step combinations (and eventually dance phrases). RaNote puts the steps for two dancers, with the music, on a stave:

Example of *paso basico* (basic step)

C	1	2	3	4	5	6	7	8
D								
M	R-	LS	RF	L+	Rs	L+	RS	Ls
W	L+	RS	LB	R-	Lf	R-	LS	Rs

Compás line describes music phrases: typically eight counts.
Description line is used for any notes about the dance/couple.
A dividing line separates the context lines above and steps below.
Man's dance line describes the leader's steps.
Woman's dance line describes the follower's steps.

It is always better to reduce the writing as much as possible. This can be done using assumptions, as previously mentioned. Here are some assumptions (for the stave), to reduce the above:

- On the **M**an's line, if there is no '…where' symbol, assume the step is taken straight towards partner (i.e. **+**).
- On the **W**oman's line, if there is no '…where' symbol, assume the step is taken with the man (*seguir* to follow, or *espejo*).
- If it is obvious which foot is moving (we assume the feet alternate), then the symbols **L** or **R** can be omitted. This is at the writer's discretion, as long as it is simple yet clear for the reader.

Applying these assumptions, the previous step combination reduces to:

Example of reduction with assumptions of: *paso basico*

C	1	2	3	4	5	6	7	8	
D	{				}	{Resolución }			The steps are
M	R-	S	RF	L	s	L	RS	s	simple and
W	L	R	L	R	f	R	L	s	complete!

The steps are clear, simple and complete. The symbols are easy to scan when read. For example, at a glance, the lower case symbols correspond to half-distance steps (see counts 5 and 8).

Dance phrases

At last, with music, steps and step combinations clearly described, we can now write the phrasing. The Description line is used for writing dance phrases (and other notes). Dance phrases are enclosed in brackets *{...}*, in italics for clarity, framing the movement or energy. Two phrases are in the above example. The second phrase/ step combination has a name: *Resolución*. Dance phrases also have accents and highlights. Here are ways these can be expressed:

{...}   brackets frame a dance phrase. Italics for clarity.
Bold   brings emphasis to a step.
___,.......underline a <u>big</u> step, dotted underline for a s<u>mall</u> step.
!,?   movement ahead/early (!) or behind/delayed (?).
∂   **d**ynamic energy/movement.
>   continuation of the step. Frame with <...>.
[   ]   a blank space describes no movement.
Piano   like music notation, words describe moods.

Grammar

These are tools used by the writer, to make RaNote clear and legible on the page (or screen), suitable for the intended reader.

.   Full stop (.) separates different steps. Also, use multiple full stops as separators if large blank spaces (tabs and indents) cannot be done.
,   Comma (,) separates parts of the same movement.
(...),^{supr}   Use brackets, or superscript, for any other information.

Examples of grammar:

LS.R.c   Shows three steps: 1) **L**eft **S**ide. 2) **R**ight, towards partner (assumed). 3) Left (assumed re context) **c**ollects.
@b,RF   A back cross collect, before a **R**ight **F**orwards step. This can also be written ^{@b}**RF** superscript clarifies priorities.

Finally, remember to write economically, reducing where possible. It's easy to over-describe Tango, with all its detail! Allow the reader to create their own interpretation of what you have written...

Examples of steps

Example 1: Counts 1-4 are walking (forwards for the man). The s steps on count 5 and 6 are two close steps with changes of weight (chg weight), onto alternate feet. Note the reduction with assumptions mentioned previously (no + and − symbols needed and not all L's and R's, as the feet are assumed to alternate).

C	1	2	3	4	5	6	7	8
D	walk			>	chg weight			
M	L	R	L	R	s	s		
W	R	L	R	L	s	s		

Example 2:

C	1	2	3	4	5	6	7	8
D	man leading forwards ochos			>				
M	€					>		
W	LF	RF	LF	RF	LF	s		

Example 3:

C	1	2	3	4	5	6	7	8
D	W back ochos			>				
M	RS	LS	RS	LS				
W	LB	RB	LB	RB				

Example 4:

C	1	&	2	3	4	5	6	&	7	8
D			crossed walking				>			
M	LS	s	L	RF	L	RF	L	s	L	s
W	R		L	R	L	R	L		R	s

Example 5: Sandwich step

C	1	2	3	4	5	6	7	8
D		sandwich			<exit		>	
M	€	R=	LS=	R-	nL	Rs	L	
W	RBr			RF(↑)	LF	Rc	R	

Examples of complex steps and step combinations
Names of steps are written on the Description line, not in italics.

Example 6:

C	1	2	3	4	5	6	7	8
D			gancho					
M	RSr	€		>	Rs	L		
W	LS	RB%	@gan	LF	Rc	R		

Example 7:

C	1	2	3	4	5	6	7	8
D		barrida >						
M	LS	<=	RFp>		Rs	L		
W	R	LB	=RS	LF(↑)	Rc	R		

Example 8:

C	1	2	3	4	5	6	7	8
D		sacada						
M	Rb	L%	>	Rs	L			
W	Lf	RF	LF	Rc	R			

Example 9: Step combinations shown with <...> framing brackets.

C	1	2	3	4	5	6	7	8
D		< G full turn when walking				>		
M	L	RS+	LB	RS-	LS-	RF	L	s
W	R	LS	RF	L+	RS	LB	R	s

Example 10: Counting *giro* steps beyond the *paso basico* step 5 (man does Rb not Rs). These are used by some teachers.

C	1	2	3	4	5	6	7	8
D	C5	6	7	8	9>	exit		>
M	Rb	L%	R%	L%	@tap	RF%	LS	Rs
W	Lf	RF	LS	RB	LS	RF	LF	Rc

Examples of dance phrasing

These examples show how to describe dance phrasing, with accents and other features of the movement.

Example 11: Musicality, stepping on the off-beat is syncopated walking. When the steps finish on count 4 it feels like the walking ends softly. The placement of the feet happens on the off-beat, so therefore the balance points are reached on each beat. Half-time walking (every second count) is also shown.

C	1	&	2	&	3	&	4	5	6	7	8
D	<	soft walking					>< half-time walking				>
M		L		R		L	Rs		L		R
W		R		L		R	Ls		R		L

Example 12: the man starts with a larger first side step. Then, both dancers do embellishments, collecting the feet behind and in front of the standing leg. For the man, it is the right leg that does the embellishments, for the woman, it is her left leg. Musicallity, double-time walking (every half count) is shown.

C	1	2	3	4	5	&	6	&	7	&	8
D	< embellished steps			>	<double-time walking						>
M	LS	@b	@f	RF	L	R	L	R	L	R	L
W	R	@f	@b	L	R	L	R	L	R	L	R

Example 13: Curly brackets *{...}* and italics identify the dance phrasing aspects. The type of dancing is described in words (smooth dancing). The phrasing brackets show movement continuing though the close step of 4,5,6 (the movement does not stop at 5). To make this even clearer, this example uses a double dividing line, acting like music slurs. The first step starts with weight put onto Man's right and Woman's left.

C	1	2	3	4	5	6	7	8
D	*smooth dancing*			{		}		
M	nR	LS	RF	L	s	L	RS	s
W	nL	R	L	R	f	R	L	s

Example 14: Two dance phrases, set to a music phrase showing accents on beats 4 and 8. The *??* in the first dance phrase indicates a slowing down, which is the build up to the strong accent, written in **bold**. The accented steps are the close (**s**) steps on count 4. In the seond dance phrase, the man leads the woman's cross (Lf) early (€!), making her step sharper.

C	1	2	3	**4**	5	6	7	**8**
D		{	??	}		{		}
M		L	RS	**Ls**		RF	L	€!,Rs
W		R	L	**Rs**		L	R	Lf

The above second phrase can be written differently, by describing the destination instead of the leading: the M-line has no €! and the W-line has the step accented in bold **Lf** or shown to be early Lf!
The writer must choose one of these options (personally, I would prefer to use Lf! as it is the most compact).

Example 15: A volcada is danced here. The phrasing describes the movement from counts 2 until 5. The leaning happens from counts 3 until 5, with a dynamic sense to it. The woman's left free leg is sufficiently described to show that it is moving, until it is placed on count 5, into a *trabada*.

C	1	2	3	4	5	6	7	8
D		{	∅∂ volcada		>}			
M	LS	€	RB-	LS	RF	L	RS	s
W	R	L@b	@	@	f	R	L	s

Note: each row of a RaNote stave corresponds to one musical phrase, counted on the Compás line. These are grouped according to music sections (see Rasche Notation book). In contrast, dance phrases can be shorter (a few steps), or longer (extending on to the next line). However, it is usual that the dance phrases fit to, or within, the music phrases.

Rasche Notation 2 (RaNote2) en Español

La sintaxis de RaNote: "Lo que va donde".

Símbolos típicamente como "Lo que ...":

L   pie izquierda (**L**eft en inglés).
R   pie derecho (**R**ight en inglés).

Símbolos típicamente como "... va donde":

S   paso lateral/al costado (**S**ide step en inglés), apertura.
F   cruce adelante (**F**ront cross en inglés)
B   cruce atrás (**B**ack cross en inglés)

s,b,f misma dirección que **S,F,B** pero para los pasos cruzados y pequeños. Por ejemplo, cruza adelante la mujer (trabada) es **Lf**.

Símbolos que se pueden agregar:

+, −   Si es un paso hacia de la pareja, agregar **+**. Para un paso lejos de la pareja, agregar **−**.
%   los pasos entre el pareja pie.
=   toques.

Cada paso se supone que es completa: a partir de una colecta de la pierna libre / pie (lo que supone en la punto de equilibrio), su proyección y colocación, seguido por transferencia completa de peso parcial y después a ella (en este punto, el paso termina). Si uno termina el paso en uno de estos puntos, es incompleta, y puede ser descrito con:

c   **c**ollect/ recogida
p   colocación (**p**royección) de pie, sin transferencia de peso.
r   transferencia parcial de peso.
n   plena transferencia de peso.

16

Los supuestos utilizados en el pentagrama:

- En la línea del Hombre (la línea **M**), si no hay simbolo "... va donde", supongamos que es un paso hacia de la pareja (**+**).
- En la línea de la Mujer (la línea **W**), si no hay simbolo "... va donde", supongamos que la paso va con el hombre, en su dirección (seguir/ espejo).
- Si es obvio que pie está en siguiente, (**L** o **R**: los pies suplente), su símbolo se puede excluir. Esto queda a criterio del autor, para hacer la notación simple y clara para el lector.

Otros símbolos

@	describe los movimientos de la pierna libre.
¥, Ω	abrazo (**¥**) y piernas (**Ω**).
€	Marca.
Φ, Ø	eje, eje inclinado.
C, G	en sentido horario (**C**), antihorario (**G**).
↑	arriba o por encima de...

Descrito por frases de danza:

{...}	Una frase van entre paréntesis. La escritura cursiva es más fácil de ver. Frases están escritas en la línea (D Description).
Neg.	Utilizar texto Negrita para mostrar acentos.
__,......	Subrayado: paso grande o pequeño.
!, ?	El movimiento es anterior, más tarde (en relación con la pareja).
∂	la energía dinámica / movimiento.
>	continuación del movimiento. Enmarcar con <...>.

Rasche Notation 2 (RaNote2) auf Deutsch

Alle Schrittsymbole beschreiben Bewegungsziele mit der Syntax: 'Was geht Wohin'.

Typische "Was ..." Symbole:

L   Links... (Fuss).
R   Rechts... (Fuss).

Typische " .. geht wohin" Symbole:

S   Seitenschritt.
F   Vorwärts Kreuzschritt (Forward).
B   Rückwärts-Kreuzschritt (Back).

s, b, f die gleiche Richtungen wie **S**, **F**, **B**, aber für kleine Schliess-/ Kreuzschritte. Zum Beispiel, Frau Kreuzschritt (trabada) ist Lf.

Symbole die hinzugefügt werden können:

+, −   Wenn es einen Schritt zum Partner hin ist, fügen Sie **+** dazu. Für ein Schritt von dem Paar weg ist, fügen Sie **−** dazu.
%   Schritt zwischen die Füsse des Partners.
=   Kontakt.

Jeder Schritt soll vollständig sein: von einer Sammlung von freien Bein / Fuß (zum Stehfuss hin), die Projektion und die Platzierung, bis zu die vollständige Übertragung des Gewichts über des platzierten Fusses (der Schritt endet hier). Falls ein Schritt unvollständig endet, kann beschrieben werden:

c   **c**ollect / Sammlung.
p   **p**latzierung Fuß ohne Gewicht zu übertragen.
r   teilweise Übertragung des Gewichts.
n   Komplette übertragen. Des Gewichts.

Die Annahmen in der Partitur verwendet:

- Auf die Tanzline für den Mann (Linie **M**), wenn kein " .. geht wohin" Symbol vorhanden ist, heisst dieses einen Schritt zum Partner hin (**+**).
- Auf die Tanzline für die Frau (Linie **W**), wenn kein " .. geht wohin" Symbol vorhanden ist, heisst dieses Sie folgt dem Mann: Sie nimmt seiner Richtung (*seguir / espejo*).
- Wenn es offensichtlich ist, welcher Fuss als nächster Schritt wird (**L** oder **R**: die Fusse wechsen sich ab), kann dieses Symbol ausgelassen werden. Dies ist Sache des Autors, um die Notation einfach und klar für dem Leser zu machen.

Andere Symbole

@	Beschreibt Freier-Bein bewegung.
¥, Ω	Tanzhaltung/Arme (**¥**), Beine (**Ω**).
€	Führung: der Partner macht die Schritte wie geschrieben.
Φ, Ø	Achse, gekippt Achse.
C, G	Uhrzeigersinn (**C**), gegen den Uhrzeigersinn (**G**).
↑	nach oben oder oben ...

Beschriebung von Tanzphrasen:

{...}	Eine Phrase is mit Klammern eingerahmt. Kursive Schrift ist einfacher zu erkennen. Tanzphrasen werden meistens auf die Description (D) Linie beschrieben.
Fett	Fettschrift kann Akzente bezeichnen.
__,......	Unterlinie: grosser, oder kleiner Schritt.
!, ?	Bewegung ist früher, später (relativ zum Partner).
∂	dynamische Energie / Bewegung.
>	Forsetzung der Bewegung. Eingerahmt mit **<...>**.

1 _____

Dance: _____

Dancers: _____

Event: _____

Music: _____

Web: _____

Notes: _____

_____

_____

_____

_____

_____

_____

_____

_____

C
D
M
W
1 2 3 4 5 6 7 8

C
D
M
W
1 2 3 4 5 6 7 8

C
D
M
W
1 2 3 4 5 6 7 8

C
D
M
W
1 2 3 4 5 6 7 8

C
D
M
W
– 1 – 2 – 3 – 4 – 5 – 6 – 7 – 8 –

C
D
M
W
– 1 – 2 – 3 – 4 – 5 – 6 – 7 – 8 –

C
D
M
W
– 1 – 2 – 3 – 4 – 5 – 6 – 7 – 8 –

C
D
M
W
– 1 – 2 – 3 – 4 – 5 – 6 – 7 – 8 –

C
D
M
W

C
D
M
W

C
D
M
W

C
D
M
W

1   2   3   4   5   6   7   8

		1	2	3	4	5	6	7	8
C									
D									
M									
W									

		1	2	3	4	5	6	7	8
C									
D									
M									
W									

		1	2	3	4	5	6	7	8
C									
D									
M									
W									

		1	2	3	4	5	6	7	8
C									
D									
M									
W									

C
D
M
W

1 2 3 4 5 6 7 8

C
D
M
W

1 2 3 4 5 6 7 8

C
D
M
W

1 2 3 4 5 6 7 8

C
D
M
W

1 2 3 4 5 6 7 8

C
D
M
W

C
D
M
W

C
D
M
W

C
D
M
W

C
D
M
W

C
D
M
W

C
D
M
W

C
D
M
W

1   2   3   4   5   6   7   8

2 _____

Dance: _____

Dancers: _____

Event: _____

Music: _____

Web: _____

Notes: _____

_____

_____

_____

_____

_____

_____

_____

_____

C
D
M
W
1 2 3 4 5 6 7 8

C
D
M
W
1 2 3 4 5 6 7 8

C
D
M
W
1 2 3 4 5 6 7 8

C
D
M
W
1 2 3 4 5 6 7 8

C
D
M
W

1 2 3 4 5 6 7 8

C
D
M
W

1 2 3 4 5 6 7 8

C
D
M
W

1 2 3 4 5 6 7 8

C
D
M
W

1 2 3 4 5 6 7 8

C		1		2		3		4		5		6		7		8	
D																
M																
W																

C		1		2		3		4		5		6		7		8	
D																
M																
W																

C		1		2		3		4		5		6		7		8	
D																
M																
W																

C		1		2		3		4		5		6		7		8	
D																
M																
W																

C
D
M
W

C
D
M
W

C
D
M
W

C
D
M
W

1   2   3   4   5   6   7   8

C
D
M
W

C
D
M
W

C
D
M
W

C
D
M
W

C
D
M
W

| | 1 | 2 | 3 | 4 | 5 | 6 | 7 | 8 |

C
D
M
W

C
D
M
W

C
D
M
W

Notes

RaNote choice of symbols

Symbols are chosen to be easy to remember and as text symbols familiar and can be written by hand and computers (without extra software). They are either abbreviations of words or pictographic:

Symbols L,R,S,B,F,s,b,f,c,p,e,C are abbreviations of words.
Symbols in capitals S,B,F are full steps.
Symbols in lower case s,b,f,c,p,r,n are small steps/ parts of a step.
Symbol r is half the shape of symbol n.
Symbol ¥ looks like arms, Ω like legs, = like two together.
Symbol € looks like an embrace, % like a step between.
Symbols @ and c look similar. Both are free leg movements.
Symbol ∂ has a **d**ynamic shape and abbreviates the word.
Symbols Φ,Ø look similar, with an axis straight or leaning.
Symbols +,-,(…), have familiar meanings.
Symbols C,G look similar: G looks like an anticlockwise arrow.

Changes in Rasche Notation 2

Revisions in RaNote2 (July 2010) are made since the 'Rasche Notation' book. These are improvements and simplificaions. These changes are: Clock directions, are no longer used. Symbol **s** replaces # without clock directions. The symbols **s**, **b** and **f** replace # with clock directions (or with clock directions in brackets). Symbols **+ –** are now used. Symbols **r** and **n** replace ∩ and Π. Symbol **C** replaces C+, and **G** replaces C-. Symbol ¥ is now also used in place of T to describe torsion. Symbol **S** can now be used instead of $ pivot side step. Symbol **e** can now be used instead of f for *firulete* (**e**mbellishment).

Further information

For information about original concepts behind Rasche Notation, please see the book 'Rasche Notation' ISBN 978-0-9561489-0-2. It covers many notation issues in depth, together with examples.

See the website www.RascheNotation.com for all developments updates and news are posted on this website. You can also join and contribute to the discussion forums.

www.ingramcontent.com/pod-product-compliance
Lightning Source LLC
Chambersburg PA
CBHW051300170526
45165CB00004B/1795